GIANTS AND DEMONS

Putana the Poisoned-Milk Demoness

SHUBHA VILAS

Om KIDZ
An imprint of Om Books International

Putana was a she-demon with big, sharp teeth protruding out of her mouth and an evil face. She had long hair, sharp, dirty nails and knew black magic. She also loved to kill newborn babies.

When Kansa, the King of Mathura learnt that Krishna had taken birth on Earth and would be the cause of his death, he panicked. He wanted to kill Krishna at any cost, and at once. His wicked mind hatched a plot. He at once contacted Putana and ordered her to kill every baby that was born in the last ten days in and around the kingdom of Mathura.

The wicked Putana was delighted at Kansa's request.

Putana transformed herself into a beautiful woman. She reached Gokula. The villagers were enchanted by her extraordinary beauty and began to follow her. They whispered among themselves that this must surely be the Goddess of Fortune who had come down to Earth to bless the babies of Gokula.

No one bothered to ask her who she really was and what her intention in entering their village was. They trusted her completely.

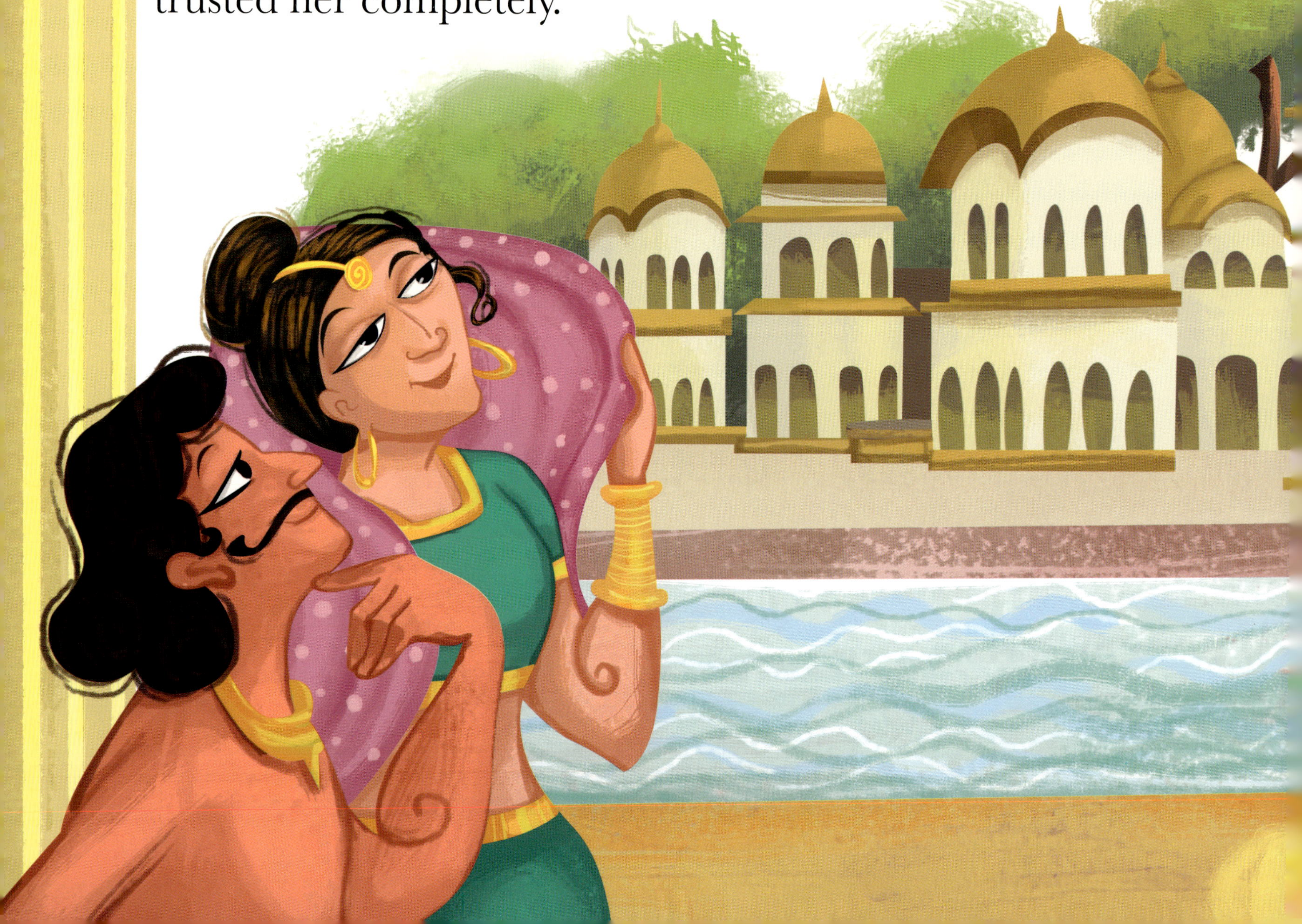

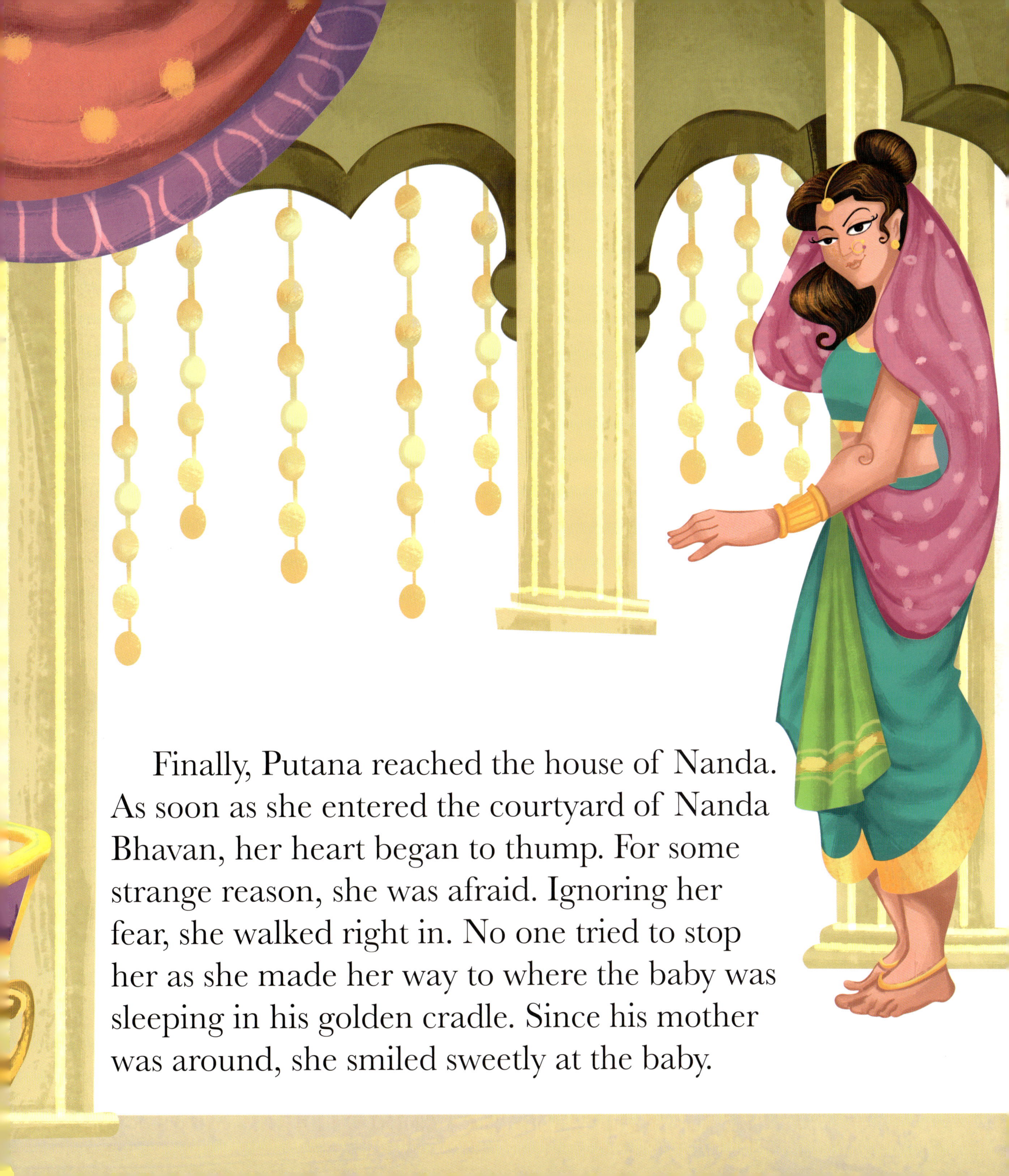

Finally, Putana reached the house of Nanda. As soon as she entered the courtyard of Nanda Bhavan, her heart began to thump. For some strange reason, she was afraid. Ignoring her fear, she walked right in. No one tried to stop her as she made her way to where the baby was sleeping in his golden cradle. Since his mother was around, she smiled sweetly at the baby.

At that very moment, little Krishna opened his eyes and stared at her. Putana carefully held the baby in her arms and placed one poison-smeared nipple in his mouth.

No longer did she remain the beautiful woman who had enchanted everyone. She again became the fearsome, ugly demoness that she actually was.

Putana had thought that the baby would soon turn blue with the poison and lie dead in her arms. But Baby Krishna's complexion was already a glowing blackish blue.

Suddenly, she felt the baby suckling her with great force. It was a type of force that was pulling out her very life from within her body. Milk was long gone, poison was long gone, and now her life itself was being pulled out forcibly by that innocent-looking baby.

With all her strength, Putana tried to forcibly push away the child. She yelled and screamed. The villagers of Gokula, the very people who had admired her earlier, were now shrieking and running away from her in great fear.

The pain was increasingly becoming unbearable for Putana. Suddenly, she felt no more pain. In a moment, all the pain had vanished.

Lifeless, she fell to the ground with a loud thud. Crushed under her were numerous trees and plants. Playing on her body was that innocent little blue boy who was the cause of her death.

Putana was immediately transported to another world, the spiritual world where she was given the role of a nurse. Though she had come to destroy him, Krishna only focussed on the fact that she nursed him with her milk. Keeping that in mind, he appointed her as his personal nurse mother in the spiritual world. Such was the kindness of Krishna.